Quest for The Lost Animals

Author: Felice S.C

Copyright © 2021 by Felice S.C

All rights reserved. No part of this publication may be reproduced, distributed, or transmitted in any form or by any me without prior written permission. Publisher's Note: This is a work of fiction. Names, characters, places, and incidents a product of the author's imagination. Locales and public names are sometimes used for atmospheric purposes. resemblance to actual people, living or dead, or businesses, companies, events, institutions, or locales is entirely coincident
Text copyright 2021 Felice S.C
Illustrations copyright Felice S.C
All reserved. Published by Right Side Publishing
Please contact the author by e-mail below for permissions and speaking events.
feliciacauley@ymail.com
Published in the US
Cover design
Editor Felicia Cauley
Project Manager
Robert Cauley
Quest for the Lost Colors
ISBN-9781955050128.
Library of Congress Control Number: 2021906050

DEDICATION

Dedicated to MiMi and Papa's Grandsix

Today Aubrey seemed sad during playtime. When Acesyn asked her the reason behind her sadness, she replies, "Yesterday I had a terrible dream. I was in my dream forest to meet my animal friends but non of them were there."
"Where could they go?" little Roman asks.
"I don't know, maybe they got lost" Aubrey replies with sadness.

"I have an idea!" Acesyn exclaims with a big smile on his face. "Let's find the animals together!"
"Do you have a plan?" Ailey asks in wonder to which Acesyn nods. "Of course, tonight we will all go to Aubrey's dream forest and look for the animals! They will surely come back!"
"We should go to bed early tonight then!" Aubrey says with a small smile.

They went to sleep and dreamed they were in the grasslands. All of them were wearing hunting hats and uniforms. "What place is this?" Roman asks. "Hmmm...We are in Africa." Acesyn informs holding a map. "What animals do we see in Africa?" Ailey inquires. "Let's see, we have Lions, Cheetahs, African Elephants and Rhinoceros here" Aubrey reads out from an encyclopedia.

"Let's find Mr. Lion first" Roman suggests and everyone nodded at him. They began searching for the 'king of jungle' a powerfully built cat. "Look over there!" Ailey says pointing to the rocks and there sat the majestic beast. "Mr. Lion won't you come back?" Aubrey asks, but the animal ignores her. "You have to use its Spanish name, Aubrey" Acesyn says before going near the beast. "Hello León. Will you come back to Aubrey's forest with us"
"If you promise to feed me meat, then I will come" The Lion says jumping down from the rock and picking up Ailey to have her sit on his back before going to the forest.

The little ones bade León and Ailey goodbye before they continued their search. "Let's head to Austra now. Australia is famous for its Kangaroos and Koalas" Aubrey reads out "Oh and Crocodiles" "I am scared of crocodiles" Roman shivers. "Cocodrilos aren't that scary but fine; we will go and look for the Kangaroos first then," Acesyn says.

...ngaroos live in the Eastern part of Australia. In grasslands, we can find the Red Kangaroos" Aubrey ...orms. "Let's go to these grasslands then" Acesyn nods. When the kids reached the plains of Australia, ...y were surprised to see groups of kangaroos jumping around. "Whoa! They're like big rats with ...kets!" Roman awes in wonder. "Right? Let me ask them to come back" Acesyn says going forward ... Canguro. Can I ask you to come back to Aubrey's forest?"
...you can provide us with vast grasslands where we can play then we will come back" The Kangaroo ...lies. "It is a deal then!" Acesyn shakes hands with the kangaroo and it picks up Roman, putting him ...de the pocket. "We will go back then!" They waved.

In the mountain woodlands of Europe, Acesyn and Aubrey searched for the brown bears. "They should around here." Aubrey hums as she walks in the woods. "I think I saw something" Acesyn says as he run towards a tree and falls on his rear in surprise when he encounters a huge brown bear, sitting behind tree. "The Spanish name of Bear is Soportar." Aubrey says as she helps Acesyn up and pats the bear o his head. "Soportar, will you come with us to my forest?"
"Do you have berries?" The bear asks. "We have plenty of berry bushes in my forest" Aubrey replies "Then I will come with you" And then Aubrey accompanied the bear back to her forest.

...en Acesyn reached Aubrey's dream forest, he found Ailey, Roman and Aubrey already there with the ...nals. The Canguros are jumping through the grasslands. The Soportar is sitting near a bush and eating ...ries. The León is resting under the shade of trees. The Guacamayo flies to sit on the apple tree. ...of them were happy to be back in Aubrey's forest.

Now it was only Acesyn left and he was assigned to find Aubrey's parrot. He went to South America's wild and he could already hear the screeching of parrots. "Guacamayo I am here to take you back to Aubrey's forest" He says loudly by using his hands as a microphone. "Woah! Aubrey's forest" A voice comes from behind and on the tree, there perched a scarlet macaw. "Does Aubrey's forest have seeds and fruits?"
"Yes! We have it all" Acesyn reassures and the macaw comes down to sit on his shoulder "Let's go!"

"...t time, let's get all of the animals back" Aubrey says with a big smile, happy to have her friends back. "... of course but for now we have to go back. The sun must be rising soon." Acesyn replies as everyone ... hands together and before they realized it, they had dreamed the same dream and woke up at the ... time to a brand new day.

A bird that kept pecking his head woke Acesyn up. Disturbed, Acesyn sat upon the grass. "What is it?" He yawns, stretching his arms. The other kids were woken up as well before the sparrow flew up to perch on the branch. "I am Restore and I need your help, children."
"It can talk!" Roman exclaims his astonishment. "Yes I can, I am a talking sparrow. I need your help to find the lost animo this forest, will you help me?" Restore asks. "We would love to help you!" Aubrey answers without a second thought. She loved animals. She can't leave someone in need like that. All the little ones agreed as well.

"So, what is the plan?" Ailey asks as Restore flies down holding the map in his mouth.
"We have to travel to the different continents to find my animal friends." The talking sparrow replies.
"How many animals do we have to look for?" Roman asks curiously. "Seis" Restore says. "Seis means six, Roman." Acesyn translates and the younger boy nods. "Can you tell us the names of your friends?" Ailey asks.
"Of course, my friends for whom we have to look for are; Hipopótamo, Pavo real, Leopardo, Elefante, Panda, Búho."
"Hippopotamus, Peacock, Leopard, Elephant, Panda, and Owl," Acesyn repeats but in English.

"Where can we find Hipopótamo?" Aubrey asks the sparrow. "They live in Africa. We should head there first" The talking b replies. The children then started their journey towards East Africa where Hippos live. When they reached the place, they looked for a river and there they found the herbivore animal. "Hipopótamo!" Acesyn calls as the little ones ran towards the animal which was playing in the water. "Oh Hipopótam, will you come with us to a new forest?" Aubrey asks
"Do you have plants and grass for my meals and a river for my baths?" Hipopótamo answers with a question.
"Yes, we do!" Roman chirps. "Then I will come." The beast replies and comes along with the group.

...pards- I mean Leopardos are found in Africa too. Why don't we look for them?" Ailey suggests. "Leopardos are like big ... Aubrey tells Roman who seems excited. "I love cats!" Roman cheers. "Leopardos live in the sub Saharan Africa. Let's head ..." Restore instructs and then the group heads towards the south of Sahara. When they reached the grassy plain, they ...d a leopard sitting on the tree. "Isn't it a Guepardo" Ailey hums. "No, guepardos have a circle or oval patterns, meanwhile ...ardos have rose patterns" Aubrey explains. "Oh, I see" Ailey hums. "Leopardo, will you come with us?" Roman asks. ...you have high trees and hares for me?" Leopardo asks. "Yes," Ailey replies. "Then I will accompany you," The big cat says, ...ping down to join in.

The next animal they had to find was Elephant- Elefante. They're also found in Africa. This average 6-meter tall animal is roaming the Savannas of Africa. "Oh Look!" Restore chirps as the group spotted the huge animal near the river.
"It has such big ears" Roman awes. "And such beautiful tusks" Acesyn adds. "Oh Elefante, please come with us," Ailey asks
"Do you have fruits for me?." The animal asks. "Yes, we have plenty of banana and apple trees!" Aubrey replies.
"Then I will be your friend," The Elephant says, picking up Roman by his trunk and putting him on his back.

little ones then traveled to Asia. "Pandas are found in the Southwest of China, They're big black and [whi]te bears but they're an endangered species now," Restore informs as he flies over them. "Look over [the]re!" Roman, who was sitting on the elephant, points. When everyone followed the pointing, they found a [bea]r sitting down on the grass, eating bamboo sticks. "Mr. Panda, come with us!" Acesyn says, extending his [han]d to the bear. "Do you have bamboos for me?" The panda bear asks. [" W]e do" Acesyn nods. "Then I will come with you," The bear says, rolling to the group.

After befriending the Panda, the kids went into a coniferous forest to look for the owl. "Búhos make th cavities in trees their home. Look for tall treea" Restore says, perching on the tusk of Elephant. "Come here," Ailey says standing by a huge tree with a deep cavity. "Excuse me, is someone in there?" Acesyn knocking on the tree trunk. "What do you kids want?" A sleepy voice comes from the cavity before a he pops out. It was an owl! "Mr. Búho, we want you to come and live with us" Aubrey suggests. "Will I get a nest and insects and beetles to eat?" Búho asks. "We will arrange it for you" Acesyn reassures. "Alright then." Búho flies and sits down on Panda's head.

...r Asia, they traveled to India to befriend the majestic bird, Peacock. "It is an extremely beautiful ... with colorful feathers," Restore says as the children and animals reached the bushlands. There they ...d the big beautiful birds running around. "Pavo real! Please join us," Restore invites. "I eat fruits and ...s. Do you have them prepared for me?" Pavo real asks. "Yes, we have plenty of fruits and seeds, ...store replies. And then the peacock joins the group as well.

All the animals and the kids went back to their forest. The pavo real enjoyed running in the grasslands and eating seeds. Búho became comfortable in the cavity of a big tree. Panda settled in the bamboo forest to chew on the sticks. Leopardo climbed a tree to sleep on its branch. Elefante entertained itself by bathing in the river. Hipopótamo accompanied the Elefante as well.

"Thank you, my friends, I wouldn't have been able to find them all if it wasn't for your help. I am truly indebted," Restore shows his appreciation. "You're welcome, Restore. Let's play with the animals together now?" Acesyn suggests and everyone seemed to love the idea. After this, the children played with the animals; enjoying their sweet little dream.

www.ingramcontent.com/pod-product-compliance
Lightning Source LLC
Chambersburg PA
CBHW061108070526
44579CB00011B/183